A SALES CULTURE FOR LAW FIRMS

The Missing Link In Business Development

Three Aspects of Business Development

Marketing

Sales

Excellent Client Service

Client Service/Sales Teams

Client Service/Sales Teams

Rick Santangelo

ISBN: 1-4392-5885-6
ISBN-13: 9781439258859

Visit www.booksurge.com to order additional copies.

Table of Contents

Dedication

First and foremost, I dedicate this book to my wife, Maria, and our three daughters, Andrea, Danielle and Rachel. They have motivated and inspired me for over the past 35 years. Even though our daughters are grown and on their own, they, along with my wife, continue to be the light of my life.

I would also like to thank every client I have ever had. Without question, even the more "challenging", each taught me something. I obviously have had some terrific mentors along the way. However, until you experience the challenge first-hand, the success - in real time, in front of a client - it is only a classroom experience.

Lastly, I thank God and all his blessings. Growing up with a wonderful family and having tremendous friends has given me a solid foundation of support. Living in the greatest country on this earth has given me many opportunities, and I am grateful.

Introduction

A Practice Group Leader at my law firm recently asked me to find a book or article (s) that clearly defines the concept of "sales" in law firms today. I thought this would be an easy task, to simply reach out to one of our library researchers to provide me with a quick answer. But to my surprise, my quest for that one answer continues to this day.

Yes, many articles exist on business development, but nothing definitive on the specific subject of sales. Every time I thought I found something on sales, pertaining to law firms, it turned out to be a hybrid marketing piece of one form or another, under the business development umbrella. So I've written this book, a clear and simple guide for those who have faced the same dilemma.

This book quickly answers the question of why you need a sales effort (not a sales force), and then establishes a framework to move that effort forward. I will define the role of **sales** within your **business development** efforts and how sales interacts with **marketing** and **client service,** and the impact you can expect from leveraging the three in forming a cohesive business development strategy.

Introduction

For clarification, I define Business Development as your overall umbrella go-to-market initiative with the three primary elements that comprise this effort - Marketing, Sales and Client Service. I provide more details on this later, but sometimes business development definitions refer to sales specifically and sometimes as the overall effort. So for simplicity sake, let's just refer to sales as sales, and your overall go-to-market efforts will be called business development.

I wrote this book with different audiences within your firm in mind. These include Practice Group(s), Geographic and Firm leadership, and lawyers wanting to foster 'rainmaking' within their firm who have not had a sales framework defined to assist them and share with their colleagues. Also, your marketing and business development people who are seeking to take their impact to the next level by incorporating sales. This book will also clearly explain what sales is all about, how it fits within your firm's business structure and business model, and why it's not just a passing fad.

This book is meant to be a quick read - not to necessarily make you an expert on the subject, but provide insights on the best ways to approach the market and to give you a better sense of where sales fits within your business development efforts. At the end of each chapter you will find some questions designed to be thought-starters for you and those around you. Your answers will emphasize key principles and help guide your investment in a sales effort. And if you have already begun to develop a sales initiative, this book will provide you a benchmark from which to measure your efforts.

Throughout this book, you will see three recurring themes that a sales process is ideally suited to address:

1. ADAPTING TO CHANGE

The rapid pace and way with which legal services are purchased seems to be accelerating. I don't have to tell you this. This constant change not only adds risk to your marketing model, but more critically, to your business model. Even as general economic conditions start to improve, having a sales process in place will help you now, as well as enable your firm to quickly capture lost revenue and market share as budgets return.

2. RELATIONSHIPS

There is simply no substitute for strong relationships. The legal field is now, and will always be, a relationship business. It is no longer enough to simply be a good lawyer who socializes professionally and personally with your clients. You now need to know their business and show the value you bring by helping them achieve their business and legal objectives. That all adds up to strong business relationships.

3. JUST-IN-TIME COACHING

Applying the basics within this book is a solid roadmap to assist lawyers who want a consistent approach to growing their business. This "quick read" gives you the opportunity to refine your sales approach, and refer back when needed. No doubt a number of lawyers within your firm genuinely want to become rainmakers - they just don't know how. They might get frustrated after a few attempts at sales, and aban-

Introduction

don the effort entirely. Or maybe they're just not willing to do things differently or attempt something new, if it brings a possible risk of failure. This book provides the guidance to help avoid that unnecessary frustration.

Having a plan in place that helps coach your lawyers on "what" to sell, "whom" to sell to and "how" to sell in the most efficient manner will be advantageous for the individual and the firm as a whole. Those who implement a sales process will reap the rewards and also lessen the chances of lost opportunities going forward.

QUESTIONS:

1. Within your firm, have you defined a comprehensive business development strategy incorporating the three fundamental elements; marketing, sales and client service?

2. Are your business development strategies focused on the short term (acquiring matters) or long term (building relationships), and should that balance change?

3. Is there a cohesive business development coaching strategy across the firm, or is it more of a "silo" effort?

Perspective on Reading this Book

The sales profession works in virtually every industry where it has been applied in earnest, and ultimately results in a positive return on investment (ROI). Products, no matter the sophistication or simplicity; services, including the Big Four accounting firms, Commercial Insurance, and Risk and Advisory Services etc. all possess sales functions. Some law firms have begun to take baby steps in the sales direction and have started to enjoy the success that goes with it. If you instill leadership, energy and a solid sales emphasis within your firm, you will be successful in moving your business development ROI forward.

Your lawyers do not need to transform themselves into salespeople. What they do need is to understand the basics of where and how they can have an impact, and the best ways to improve their chance of success and recognition. This includes understanding why a pursuit succeeds or fails. Chances are, the impact of a sales effort will not be earth-shattering at first, but will be incremental over time. These incremental, cumulative steps will compound over 12 to 18 months and begin to become significant.

This book is all about starting on this sales journey, applying the basics, understanding the rationale, and beginning to develop the sales culture at your firm. Here is how it is organized:

Chapters 1 - 4 – These chapters deal with the early stage of defining how a sales initiative fits within your law firm. You will learn what sales is all about, what you can expect and how urgently you need a sales initiative. Please pay special attention to the setting expectations chapter. Sales aren't a magic potion for all things being challenged within business development in the legal industry. What it will do is help you address the changing market being dictated by your clients and the economy. Once you have a good sense that a sales initiative should be considered at your firm, you may move on.

Chapters 5 – 6 – You have made the decision that a sales initiative should be considered at your firm. These two chapters address the steps you should consider as you prepare to define and roll out your sales initiative. This is also meant as a foundation for discussing sales with your leadership and those lawyers who will likely participate in the sales process initially. The process overview provides you with a snapshot of what the sales process is all about. So once you begin to get buy-in, you can begin a focused and efficient effort to map out what will be needed for a successful sales initiative.

Chapters 7 - 13 – These chapters look at the tactical phase of a sales pursuit, and explain how it all works and how you apply it to individual pursuits once you identify your sales targets. In essence, you will go from concept to actual results.

Chapters 14 – 16 – These chapters bring you back to the basics of focus and follow-up. This includes maintaining momentum (communication, preparation, measurement, recognition, and a few other golden nuggets) throughout your firm.

QUESTIONS:

1. Are the changing economic realities (yours and your client's) making it more critical that you achieve an improved ROI from your business development efforts?

2. Are the demands in the marketplace dictating that you approach new and existing clients differently?

3. Is there a need today to have a better dialogue with your clients in order to address their changing demands more quickly?

1. Do I Need a Sales Initiative at my Firm?

Is it a question of **if**…or **when**?

Have you seen any of these things happening?

- The increased numbers of Requests for Proposals (RFPs)?

- Procurement departments suddenly getting involved in legal services?

- A stepped up effort toward lean and cost saving initiatives?

- CEOs directing their General Counsels to act more like business people than lawyers?

- An intense focus on fees and fee alternatives?

You can bet that these changes are significantly affecting, not only lawyers, but your client base as well. Also added to the mix is the ongoing turbulence in today's economy.

You have two choices – be reactive and let the market dictate your future – or proactive – become an early adapter and dictate your own future. Instead of waiting for the economy

Do I Need a Sales Initiative at my Firm?

to improve, you can take advantage of near-term opportunities. You'll be positioned to accelerate your sales faster than your competition once legal spending gets back on track. The best part is that most of the changes in your marketplace are non-legal in nature, so they're not difficult to implement. They are just areas that today's lawyers are not trained to handle but still need to know.

About 15 to 20 years ago, accounting firms were struggling with the same issue of building a sales culture that law firms ponder today. But what prompted the accounting firms to move in this direction was a reaction to competitive pressures. Most of the major accounting firms developed sales initiatives to act as a vehicle to implement their growth strategy built around productizing and line proliferation. They found out that this sales activity worked for them. Failure to react quickly enough affected their growth model but fortunately, for those who were behind this curve, not their business model. Their clients were not demanding it, instead it was their sense of need to grow rapidly, and their perceived value for critical mass, that propelled it.

As I performed in-depth research for this book, a number of articles were particularly telling as evidence of change. One reported that law firms, such as Kirkland & Ellis and Jones Day, are being pressured by their clients to send work overseas. With the huge wage gap between the U.S. and countries such as India, clients see this as one way of saving money.

Compounding the problem are the quickly escalating entry level salaries at law firms in the U.S. The current economy has temporarily slowed this trend, but it will again crop up once the economy turns around. The wage gap is big and getting bigger. Accounting firms have had these issues for years but have adjusted. Having an effective sales initiative in place will allow you to identify trends early on and give you time to develop solutions in a planned and organized fashion. Being proactive is better than having your clients bring this to your attention, with you being caught off guard and struggling to catch up.

In 2007 a leader in measuring trends and client satisfaction in the legal industry noted that just over 60 percent of clients have changed one of their major law firms within the past 18 months. Surprisingly, client service issues are most often mentioned as the primary reason for changing law firms, not a lack of legal expertise. If done properly, an effective sales process can also alert you early on regarding client dissatisfaction.

My sense is that the pace of change within the legal world is quickening and will continue even as the economy slowly rebounds. Meeting evolving client service demands and pricing pressures are just beginning. These will no doubt escalate as the clients (who are early adapters) show real dollar savings and start to expect client service improvements. Failure for a law firm to react will affect both your growth and business model. It is just not your competition acting differently; your clients are, too. How your services are secured, how you bill, how you are paid, how you manage projects more efficiently – are all being challenged. As a result, your business model is also adversely affected.

Do I Need a Sales Initiative at my Firm?

I once worked as a Senior Account Manager for a company in the Performance Improvement Industry. It was a great job, selling consulting services to the sales and marketing departments of Fortune 500 companies. They had big budgets and loyalty to those who helped them meet their objectives. The business changed for many of the reasons I mentioned in chapter 1. Those who adapted to change saw their businesses grow. For those that did not – their business suffered losses. Unfortunately my company was one of the those negatively affected.

The point of a sales initiative is just not to grow your revenue, but to do it efficiently and profitably. You have to understand what your clients need, and what they will and will not pay for. You have to understand their business and what they mean when they say they want creative pricing. Any law firm can go out tomorrow and grow revenue by hiring more lawyers and / or by acquiring smaller firms. But this type of growth isn't the end game unto itself.

At the end of the day, it's about ROI. In a partnership that means revenue and profit per partner. Once you see that stagnation or downturn begin, then you are stuck. If you keep doing things the same way they've always been done, the results won't change.

About 20 years ago, I had quite a bit of business with a Fortune 100 consumer products manufacturer. At the time, their retail distribution was comprised of independent dealers that made up the bulk of their sales, along with about 2,000 company owned outlets. Half of the company owned outlets were unprofitable and the company was in a cash and profit crunch.

The General Manager responsible for the company owned outlets decided that the easiest and quickest way to fix his P&L problem was to simply close most of the 1,000 unprofitable stores. He did little else, leaving the 1,000 or so profitable stores alone. A few years later sitting in the office of his replacement, (his predecessor having been fired) the new General Manager lamented the fact that they went from 2,000 stores to 1,000 profitable company owned outlets. The result? You guessed it. In the course of just over two years, half of the formerly profitable stores, became unprofitable.

The new General Manager immediately realized that his predecessor kept doing the same things. After some time, he got back to the same results, one-half the stores were still unprofitable.

The message is simple. You can't go out one day and eliminate all your marginal performers to cut costs. You also can't hire additional lawyer superstars, and then expect to grow revenue and experience real change.

If you don't genuinely change how you do business, you may get a short term spike in your metrics. But in the end you will get the same results. At best, you'll see the same profits per partner, same revenue per partner etc. And if your competition begins to adapt, even the status quo will become unreachable as the market passes you by.

The good news. Sales efforts are about opportunity, not gloom and doom. The market will change slowly, so time is on your side - as long as you don't wait too long. Make your plans to

Do I Need a Sales Initiative at my Firm?

evolve quicker than your competition. And then, as they say, "opportunity will knock."

Don't get me wrong. I'm not suggesting that sales is the only solution to your growth and profit needs. But it is a key opportunity in today's market, and perhaps a way to harvest low hanging fruit for those who take the initiative to commit now to change.

QUESTIONS:

1. Did you see buying patterns begin to change even before the economy nose-dived, and do you anticipate these changes will continue?

2. Will you be able to stay abreast of market changes real-time, and is your business development group able to identify and anticipate change or simply be reactive once change is thrust upon you?

3. Are your business development efforts the same as they were 18 months ago or are you adapting to change?

2. Sales – Setting Expectations

Before I explain the details of a sales initiative, I will first frame out what you can expect from one.

The primary objective of the sales function in a professional services firm is to thoroughly understand client trends and needs. Once you have those answers, you can efficiently align those needs with your services. This two-way conduit of business information and idea exchange isn't just legal in nature, but should address what is going on within the client's space. Gathering intelligence through sales principles is a dynamic situation that will ebb and flow throughout the year (s). It needs to be an ongoing effort, instead of a one-time event in your marketplace, industry, or geographic location.

I have worked in professional services for more than 20 years with three different firms, including my current position. At each firm, we were engaged with what salespeople call "complex sales," where you need to address various elements and influences before you can position yourself to win. In today's world, a lawyer can no longer win business based on reputation and past experience alone. The whole sales process has become a lot more "complex".

Sales – Setting Expectations

Today, multiple "buyers" influence the buying decision. You'll discover that many different variables need to be addressed before you can gain significant, incremental recurring revenue with a new or existing client. Keep in mind that industry dynamics will change from year to year. To maintain the proper sales focus, you need a pipeline of real-time information. Let me explain.

As I began researching and writing this book, I noted that BTI Consulting Group, a leading provider of strategic research to law firms, revealed at the end of 2008 six driving trends for 2009:

1. Economic uncertainty flattens the legal market

2. In-sourcing is the new outsourcing

3. Convergence is a reality

4. Is your firm prepared to embrace the political changes ahead?

5. There are still a few bright spots in the market…is your firm in line for the work?

6. The bailout bill is a life raft for law firms

In essence, business issues exist that are non-legal and non-technical in nature. In countless industries, sales initiatives have been built to help identify these types of issues, validate whether or not they are real within your space, and then provide ideas on how to best address them. Trends 1 and 2 above threaten the current outside legal spend. The other four may somewhat jeopardize your sales efforts, but more importantly, may present opportunities for growth. If I had asked you at the beginning of 2009 the prevalence of these trends among your clients and where, would you have known? Will you know in time to take advantage of the opportunities and put in place activities to mitigate the effects of any downside issues?

As I began to finish up this book in mid 2009, BTI presented a mid-year Webinar on current trends in the legal industry. These trends continue to change rapidly, both in strategic direction, as well as in how much and where the legal spend is headed.

But by the time you read this book, the trends will change again. The important question for you to consider is whether you understand the trends and how they will affect you as you move forward. **BTI and other research firms are talking to your clients to find out the trends. You need to ask yourself how effective you are in talking to your clients and getting this information on a first-hand and timely basis?**

Have you done your homework with your clients, as a firm and not just a few individuals? Taking the opinion of just one individual can be very dangerous and sometimes misleading. You need to address their issues, mitigate the downside risks and maximize the opportunities.

In essence, you need to ask yourself what you have in place to identify and address these trends? You have two options. You can either be proactive in addressing them and get ahead of your competition, or you can wait it out and hope your firm will hang in there without any long-term damage.

Sales may not be the cure for all the market challenges you face today. But understanding the changing marketplace at an early point in the cycle, and designing your go-to-market strategies to address them are key components of a successful sales effort. This, coupled with an efficient process, will enable you to close opportunities once they are identified. The ultimate goal of a sales function is to initiate and maintain an actionable and meaningful dialogue within the marketplace.

Sales is not just about answering RFPs and the changing buying patterns and protocols. The proactive approach involves having **conversations** with your clients, directed with planned outcomes. This type of tactic keeps you ahead of your competitors.

Ten years ago, the parameters around client needs were fairly simple. Your client had a legal issue and if you were at the right place, at the right time and had the proper credentials, you had a very good chance of getting the business. If your overall business decreased, chances were, most other law firms were in a similar situation. All you had to do was wait it out.

Those days are gone.

The complex sales world has caught up to you.

Today, winning business involves more than simply being at the right place at the right time. You need to understand the client's business, their protocols, the type of billing structures they prefer, their prime criteria for buying, the type of diversity initiatives they reward…and all this intelligence is needed before you identify their legal needs.

Take a look at the RFPs that have crossed your desk lately. How many of them are about creative billing rates, number of woman and minority partners, the type of efficiencies instilled in your service model, and so on? Today, the experience of your firm and individual lawyers are the easy parts.

As fluctuating economic conditions continue to be uncertain, can you really afford to scale down your firm size and expect to scale back up quickly when the market returns? The cost of a new associate, lateral hire, and staff support continue to escalate quickly, causing the in-and-out strategy to continue to be more expensive, and is questionable whether it can be supported going forward. A sales effort should help smooth out some of those peaks and valleys.

So the expectation is fairly simple - your sales effort should reflect your understanding of the increasing complexities of client expectations and be a barometer of change within the marketplace. This will give you time to anticipate and address how you handle client change. **Chances are you have the answers – you just need to know the questions that are top-of-mind with your clients.**

QUESTIONS:

1. Do you have a process in place to monitor trends for legal needs in the marketplace real time?

2. Do you have a process in place to monitor trends of buying parameters real time?

3. **Do you have a system in place to communicate these changes throughout your firm?**

3. What is Business Development – and Where Does Sales Fit?

For the sake of clarity and discussion, let's agree that the umbrella of all "go-to-market" activities fall under what we will call Business Development. This is to avoid confusion in future terminology discussions. If you are a marketing guru reading this and don't agree with the terminology, please just hear me out for this discussion. Common sales terminology, which isn't prevalent in today's legal community will enhance the effectiveness of future conversations.

Under **Business Development** sit three elements: **Marketing, Sales and Client Service:**

Three Aspects of Business Development

Marketing

Client Service/Sales Teams

Sales

Client Service/Sales Teams

Excellent Client Service

MARKETING

Law firms have had a marketing function for some time. Brochures, collateral materials, seminars, articles, and press releases, have become a mainstay for firms to get their message out to potential clients. But in the end, defining your brand and developing contacts is what marketing should be all about.

By defining your brand, you tell people who you are - the quality of your firm, how you interact with your clients, geographic coverage, your service offerings, differentiators, and value. Your marketing materials are indicative of how you define yourself. My guess is most of your marketing materials highlight how proficient you are at being a really good lawyer. But is this really the only message you want to convey?

JKS & Company, a legal strategic client interview firm, asked General Counsels to rate their law firms on an A to D scale, where A is the highest and D is the lowest. Interestingly, only 10 percent were ranked C and D. Seventy percent received a B ranking and the A firms comprised the top 20 percent.

The difference between an A firm and a B firm was not good lawyering. It was knowing the General Counsel's business and applying that knowledge to become a valued advisor focusing on bringing real value to the client relationship through understanding and service.

If every General Counsel's definition of a valued advisor with great client service and deep knowledge of the client's business were the same, this would be a simple (yet difficult) fix. But every GC is different depending on their organization, experience, and goals, so there is no simple fix. This is a tough combination that will handsomely reward the firms that figure this out, while the rest will get caught up in the everyday noise that prevents them from surging ahead. I will get to the solution in later chapters, but this is a key element to understand at the outset.

The second part of marketing is establishing contacts. Avenues such as seminars, sponsorships, bulletins, press releases, and community involvement provide a basis to begin identifying, building and cultivating relationships. Most law firms are still hesitant to cold call. Whether it is ethics, image or market concerns, it really doesn't matter. Cold calling is not going to be an accepted practice in our industry in the near future. Frankly, I think this is a good thing. Cold calls are generally a panic reaction to a sudden downturn in business conditions or outlook, and will ultimately become wasted effort.

Through marketing, you have the stimulus for establishing contacts and your brand. Once you have established your brand, transforming contacts into relationships is the starting point to transition marketing into revenue (sales). If done effectively, this puts you ahead of the game.

SALES

Two primary functions of sales in a law firm are to convert contacts into solid business relationships and to monetize your brand.

Monetizing your brand means defining, positioning and mining your relative worth in the marketplace. As a firm, as individual lawyers, will you be able to charge more or less than your competition? What is the comfort zone of what you may charge? Are you worth a 5-, 10- or 20-percent premium over other firms in your space? Do you need to discount a similar amount to get the business? If your sales support and presentation materials are only defining who you are, then you are leaving money on the table. They must also define your worth and ultimate value to your clients. Your worth is a factor of experience and results. How well you qualify your experience and how proficient you are at quantifying your results will determine whether you will earn a premium or need to discount in order to get the preferred business.

QUALIFY YOUR EXPERIENCE

Qualifying your experience isn't just about describing your matter involvement. It is about the elements of success you achieved within these types of matters. What were the building blocks of your success? Are there some common threads that make you most effective across the spectrum of your experience, or is it just unique to a few of your matters?

QUANTIFY YOUR RESULTS

Quantifying your value through your results may be a challenge. You may not be able to do it in each and every matter, but at some level you need to consider why you are a better value than your competition. It may be through measurable success in practices such as litigation and tax controversy or perhaps how your methodology exceeds that of your competition.

The second aspect of sales is transforming contacts into revenue. Contacts are a natural outcome of your marketing efforts. You can't help but make them. It is the quality of your contacts, and what you do with them, that separate the top 20 percent A players from the B players. Moving relationships forward is the key to transforming contacts into revenue. We will talk more about that later, but make no mistake - we live in a relationship world.

Customer Relationship Management (CRM) systems are tremendous aides when used appropriately. But you should consider them only an aide – you are the one who should take the lead in mining your contacts. If they do not fit the ideal profile of whom you would like as clients, then you need to change marketing strategies. But somewhere within you or your firm's contact lists are, no doubt, some excellent contacts that fit the profile of the clients you want.

So in the end, sales is first about monetizing your brand, crystallizing your relative worth in the marketplace, positioning yourself to maximize that worth. Define yourself so you can play and be paid with the top 20 percent. Secondly, identify your primary contacts that fit the profile of companies or individuals with whom you want to do business. Then you can develop a process to turn those relationships into revenue.

Client Service Teams

One other point is the issue of **Client Service Teams**. Once you obtain a client, you need to focus on Client Service but you can't forget the marketing and sales aspects of business development. Basic sales concepts fit very well in this environment. Look at the model on page 13 and you see that Business Development is a continuous loop. This applies to current clients as well.

A certain amount of pride exists that drives all of us to want to provide excellent client service as a stand-alone output. However, the primary objective of a client service team (from a business standpoint) is to protect the brand and grow the relationship. Most client service team meetings seem to revolve primarily around client service. They sprinkle in a few marketing functions and forget a key component of the business development model - sales.

Talk to some of your largest clients and ask how they position their client service teams with their key customers. They probably call or position them more as Account Management teams, but the function and objectives should be nearly identical. These include:

- Growing your understanding of the client

- Building relationships throughout the organization

- Identifying needs and issues, not just functional needs, but industry, company and business division needs, goals and objectives

The goal should be to understand the client better than any of your competitors. Sales are a primary activity within the Account Management or client service function. It will continue to be because sales is ultimately the bridge between client needs, your services and the most efficient way of growing the relationship.

CLIENT SERVICE

Regardless of the product or service you are supplying, no sales or marketing organization in the world can make up for poor client service. A significant difference exists between client satisfaction and client loyalty, or as some products companies call it, "customer or client delight."

A satisfied customer only stays with you until a better mousetrap comes along - then they are gone. A delighted, loyal customer sees a better mousetrap and first asks if you can meet or exceed the new mousetrap's value and then gives you the opportunity to do so. You may not always be able to meet or exceed the competition and might occasionally lose. But in the end, your client knows that life is a marathon and not a sprint. Anyone can be undercut or outperformed by someone else at any one moment in time. But if your relationship is solid enough, your client will recognize that a long-term working relationship is far more efficient than a series of "one-offs". Even if you miss out on a current piece of business, the next time around, the opportunity will be yours.

Undoubtedly, with procurement groups now getting in the mix, less and less loyalty will exist. They only measure price and concessions. However, truly loyal customers will continue to be your most profitable, and potentially your highest growth clients. Ample numbers of them exist, even with procurement departments lurking nearby. You need to take advantage of the benefits of a loyal customer whenever possible. This effort will make up for those who disappear due to company procurement policies, service breakdowns, and being bought and sold.

What is Business Development – and Where Does Sales Fit?

Measuring client loyalty versus client satisfaction

There is an old adage, "If you can't measure it you can't manage it." If you are not measuring client loyalty, then why even pretend that it is a priority for your firm? You wouldn't go through life without measuring partner revenue and profits, how much you spend as a firm and how much revenue you generate. **What you measure is an indicator of what you value.** There is a difference between client satisfaction and client loyalty. You should be measuring both.

For client loyalty, the first thing you need to do is determine exactly what constitutes a loyal client. It goes beyond the soft measures of client satisfaction. Take into consideration how much of their legal spend you have, the quality of your relationships up and down the line (not just with the GC), how long they've been a client, how many practice areas they give you and their profitability as a client. After identifying these measurements of client loyalty, you then need a system to measure the "it" for client satisfaction. It can be informal or formal, costly or not, but you need to do it. Word of mouth or gut feel of how you are performing does not address the issue. **It only makes the disappointment of losing a customer a greater probability.**

Referrals versus references

Retention rates, growth rates with current clients, and referrals - not just references - are critical client service measurements. They clearly indicate whether you are maximizing the ROI from your marketing and sales efforts. Satisfied clients provide nice references. A client reference is someone you may call and ask if they will praise your lawyers and your firm to a potential client. Loyal clients provide referrals without hesitation. A referral client, as a course of his or her everyday business, suggests you and your firm without prompting. It happens when you're not there, and carries much more weight than a reference.

MEANINGFUL, MEASURABLE, MOVABLE

The acid test that any or all of the three Business Development elements mentioned previously are significant to your firm is to answer positively that these three initiatives are meaningful, measurable and movable:

- Meaningful – Is there a significant consequence to doing or not doing it?

- Measurable – Have you defined success and measured progress towards achieving that success?

- Movable – Are your goals challenging but achievable? They may be a stretch, but can it be done?

QUESTIONS:

1. How meaningful are each of your three elements of business development; marketing, sales, and client service?

2. Do you measure ROI for each of these elements?

3. How has the dynamics of a loyal client changed over the past two years, and how will you anticipate additional changes over the next two years?

4. Sales – The End Game - Relationships, Relationships, Relationships

Some may argue that the end game of a sales initiative is all about revenue. But revenue for revenue sake is not supportive of a sustainable sales process. It is a short term fix, not a long-term solution. Rather, sales in a professional services organization is about building **relationships** that lead to recurring revenue and the ability to mine a lifetime value of a client.

Relationships come in three varieties; Cold, Warm and Advisory:

- **Cold** – These are contacts you know, but barely. It might be someone you met on a few occasions but never really followed up with either socially or through a business setting. They're basically a name on a contact list. These generally are non-clients but sadly, occasionally they are clients.

- **Warm** – These are contacts with whom you regularly interact, either socially or from a business perspective. Within your firm these are generally clients, perhaps even good clients. For the most part, you share their business with other firms and have a good relationship with them overall.

- **Advisory** – These clients are generally your most profitable. They rely on you to help them make decisions. They value the knowledge you have about their company and the investment you have made to be in that position. They reach out to you for input on legal services needed to address business issues. In essence, you are in a position to help frame up their legal spend rather than simply respond to a request to perform certain services.

  Before doing anything in certain areas, they first pick up a phone and ask you. If a legal competitor comes in with a great idea, they run it past you to get your input whether or not it will work. Then they ask if you might have a better idea. They may reward your competitor with the business for being proactive, to prevent discouraging future ideas, but you are neither surprised nor shortchanged for a chance to give your opinion and respond. And if an unrelated matter comes down the road the day after they award business to your competitor, they still come back to you as a first choice on the next matter.

Advisory relationships are the end game. Profitable clients with significant recurring revenue generally reside here. These clients want you to be profitable. They value the relationship with you as well. If you are not profitable, they know you won't be around very long. And they want you around; hence they want you to be profitable.

Advisory relationships also provide two other key components.

One, they will be your best test market. These clients are more apt to accept your suggestions and agree to your proactive service offers. The buying threshold here will not be nearly as high as with a Cold or even Warm relationship, because the client will know you have already asked yourself the tough questions to avoid jeopardizing the relationship. As a result you save significant time and money that would have been invested in selling new ideas to them. Frankly, at this stage, you aren't really selling. Proactive ideas are agreed to as a course and outcome of business conversations, and not selling situations.

The second big advantage of an advisory relationship is to keep you in the premier referral network. A referral source is different from a reference as discussed previously.

So whether you are talking to your own client, a firm client that has not engaged you or your practice, or a non-client, your objective is to move these relationships forward. But sales isn't just about moving the relationship forward, it is about doing it efficiently and predictably.

One other note on this subject - Advisory relationships are a great advantage for your clients as well. They create buying efficiencies. If they have to shop around, analyze the responses and then take on the risk of a new law firm, it will create more risk and work for your client. This is a slow process that does not get the job done over the long term.

QUESTIONS:

1. Have you focused your go-to-market objectives on building relationships?

2. Are each of your key clients moving toward an Advisory relationship?

3. Do you build into your client discussions the means and benefits of advancing your relationship?

5. Sales – Getting Started

This chapter addresses the strategic side of getting started with your sales initiative rather than the individual pursuit process. As you plan this initiative and establish a foundation upon which to build, I would suggest three overriding considerations to keep in mind as you start:

- Commit to prioritizing

- Determine goals and objectives

- Focus and follow-up

COMMIT TO PRIORITIZING

Prioritizing is important on two fronts. First, you most likely have limited time and resources within your firm to launch a successful sales effort. Secondly, you can easily proliferate the process within your firm if you can show early sales success. So getting the right people involved at the outset is critical.

You no doubt have a good understanding regarding where your greatest opportunities for growth reside. So prioritizing your initiative is really about asking yourself a few basic questions. Which practices, industry groups, and geographic locations hold the greatest potential for sustained growth and success? Keep in mind the types of clients these groups currently serve and the people within your firm who serve them. Here are some questions to help you get started:

- Where are you most likely to find clients and non clients with significant profitable and recurring revenue, in addition to the opportunity to grow to an advisory relationship? We will get to more details in developing specific criteria in "Chapter 7 – Identify," but look at where your current growth clients reside. This will give you the best insight on what client criteria to base successful sales efforts on going forward.

- Among your practice, geographic or industry groups, which individuals or groups have the discretionary time, effort and ability to be successful in developing your best opportunities for profitable, recurring revenue?

  But you have to be realistic. If a group is billing over 2,200 hours per lawyer per year, chances are they do not have the bandwidth to support a sales effort. A few may be able to carve out some time despite their workload. If they do, you can bet the hours spent on business development will be sporadic at best. Each time they begin to develop momentum; a client demand will sidetrack them. Then, weeks later, when they get back to the sales effort, they will find themselves back at ground zero.

- Do they **want** or **need** to develop new business? If I had to choose between ability and desire, give me desire any day. Some lawyers are naturally better than others when it comes to developing business. But when it comes to sales, very few performers can overcome the lack of desire with raw ability. This is no different than in the courtroom. Once people lose the drive to win, their chance of success is minimal, no matter how talented they appear.

Hopefully, your business development group, finance, and library resources can help quantify some of your instincts regarding specific areas of opportunity. Having the facts and figures will be very helpful in validating your ideas on growth potential. Fact-based selling provides the foundation that gives you the confidence to move forward. Having confidence in your priorities from the outset eliminates a lot of the dabbling that folks will want to do if not fully committed.

DETERMINE GOALS AND OBJECTIVES

Once you have prioritized a few selected areas, begin developing your objectives. As you start, you will see it's more art than science in developing the interim steps that lead to sales success. But once you define your objectives, you can begin to crystallize specific goals. Objectives in the sales arena come in two forms, activities and results.

Activities are steps taken that lead to the sale. These steps include identifying targets, qualifying them, face to face meetings, presenting a proposal etc.

Results are simply that – results or successful outcomes. How many new clients does your firm have? How much revenue has been generated? Have you reduced your client turnover ratio? How much have profits increased per client? How many more Advisory relationships have been created?

The pursuit process in the next chapter will more fully define the activities portion of this effort. A few quick examples on short-term activity objectives - engage two markets and/or two practice groups with six lawyers involved in each. Meet every six weeks with each group and identify up to 15 targets. Prioritize seven targets per group and have a probing meeting with each target. Accomplish these activities within the first 90 days – with the goal within the first year to gain three new clients.

Here is a word of warning in setting your sales objectives. If you make them too aggressive, you set yourself up for disappointment and potentially lose the momentum of your initiative. If you set them too low, you may find yourself putting in a lot of work with little results to show for your efforts. People will say "so what" and wonder if you really accomplished anything that significantly contributes to the firm.

After 90 days, do a checkpoint for progress and then expand objectives and activities as needed. Possibly consider revenue milestones over the next 12 to 18 months.

FOCUS AND FOLLOW-UP

This sales games is not, as they say, "rocket science." In the end, it is simply about focus and follow-up. If you remember only two concepts from this entire book, they should be **focus and follow-up**.

If you attend a pursuit meeting for a key target and realize that noise is beginning to take over, call a timeout and steer the meeting's attention to focus and follow-up.

Start with focus. Whether in a meeting or establishing a direction, goals or objectives, maintain the focus on what you are trying to accomplish. The goal is to avoid the noise - the distraction of indecision and push-back.

How many times have you attended a meeting, bouncing from idea to idea but not working in any discernable direction? Generally, it is because the participants don't know how to address the issues at hand, or perhaps they have another agenda. To avoid this for each meeting and step in the process, make sure your agenda clearly states the objective of moving the process to the next step. Typically, an internal sales discussion should focus on the points below. Not all points will get addressed in one meeting, but the overall direction should be evident.

Please read the caution language on page 33 to bring some perspective to the focus and follow-up questions.

Focus – the internal meeting discussions should revolve around the following:

- What are you trying to accomplish? Do you know where you are in the sales process and what you need to do to get to the next step?

- Do you know how the client buys, and his or her protocols?

Sales – Getting Started

- Do you know the client's buying criteria?

- Can you identify the buying influences?

- Do you know what the client is looking for, both legal and non legal – and not just issues, but needs?

- Can you address what they are looking for, with solid differentiators?

- What are your forms of evidence, in terms of background, experience and results?

- What is your value proposition?

- Does an opportunity exist for you to become a trusted advisor and not simply one engaged in one-off matters?

Follow-up

- How are you going to communicate with the client – get answers to the questions noted above and position the opportunity to present your story when the time is right?

- Who is going to spearhead this communication?

- What client takeaways do you need that reinforces this communication?

- What is the timing of your next steps?

- Who has overall responsibility to coordinate this effort?

- What is your strategy? Where are the touch points to support an ongoing effort to take you from a Cold relationship to a Warm one and then on to an Advisory relationship? Going from Cold to Advisory is difficult to tackle in one fell swoop. Generally it is a progression.

CAUTION: You should not expect to answer these questions in a vacuum. A methodology is needed to get there. By the end of this book, you will have the methodology to achieve success.

QUESTIONS:

1. Have you begun to identify groups and/or individuals within your firm that would benefit from a sales effort?

2. What types of goals do you want to establish going forward?

3. How have you or will you show discipline for the focus and the follow-up at each step of the process needed to succeed?

6. Pursuit Process

Once you have established your goals and objectives, and have your teams in place, it is now time to take them on the journey that we call the Pursuit Process, the tactical side of the sales equation.

Overall, the purpose of the pursuit process is to identify a very broad set of targets and narrow them down quickly and efficiently. You can now focus (there is that word again) and follow-up (the other phrase again) with your best opportunities in an efficient and effective manner. The result - increasing the odds for success and bettering your close rate thereby increasing your Business Development ROI. There are seven steps in the pursuit process under three overriding categories - **Prepare, Pursue and Proliferate**. Let me give you a quick overview of each one. Subsequent chapters will provide you with additional detail.

Under **Prepare** are the first two steps, **Identify** and **Qualify**

1. **Identify** – You have picked your team and now you're ready to begin. The first thing you will need to do is identify your targets. To do this, you have to build criteria around what your targets should look like. What will be your ideal client based on history, current emphasis and

go-forward strategy? Where do you find these targets?
Who will be your best clients going forward?

2. **Qualify** - Once you have identified your targets, how do
you quickly qualify them? Drill down a little deeper into
each company. Make sure you do your homework so you
can mitigate any surprises. Eliminate targets that don't fit
your criteria. Uncover red flags and prioritize to give you
the best chances of early success with those targets that fit
the criteria. An initial fact-finding conversation with the
prospect is also in order in this phase. Qualifying is really
about narrowing your targets to a manageable number that
gives you the best chance of success.

Under **Pursue,** there are three steps, **Solution Assessment,
Separation Strategy** and **Ask for the Sale:**

3. **Solution Assessment** – Once you have qualified your
target(s), the next step is to understand this target thoroughly, and the opportunities that exist. It is not only
about the services you can offer, but also how you will do
business with them. Once you find out how this target
operates, you may determine that they would not be a
good fit. You are better off finding this out now, instead of
after you have invested considerable time putting proposals together, with no results. Worse yet would be to find
this out after your engagement is finished and the invoice
doesn't get paid.

4. **Separation Strategy** – What will it take to separate you
from the competition and win the business? This is not
as difficult as it sounds. I think most firms, legal or not,

overcomplicate the answer to this question. How about this for an idea – let the target determine 80 percent of the optimal separation strategy.

5. **Ask for the Sale** – This is really part of the Separation Strategy step and I will explain why in Chapter 11.

Under **Proliferation**, we **Debrief** to gather intelligence and examine why and how we won, and whether we can leverage those efforts to win additional business. If we lost, we should figure out why. What did we learn? This is followed by **Next Steps**, to determine how you continue the pursuit, win or lose:

6. **Debrief** – Why did we win or why did we lose? Both internal and external conversations are helpful and especially interesting to see if they match. Always hold the internal review first, then the external. Report the findings to the team. It isn't just about what you did wrong; it's about what you did right. You will be empowered to repeat what you did well while overcoming any downsides.

7. **Next Steps:**

   - If you won, begin preparing to win the significant, recurring revenue. I am not suggesting that you immediately go out and ask for more business. But the team should be reminded of the end game and begin developing a strategy to get there.

   - If you lose, you should try to determine what went wrong and fix it, if possible. Also see if there is

> sufficient probability of an acceptable ROI going
> forward. If not, abandon the pursuit going forward.

So there you have it. It's not a very complicated process but the discipline and execution can be challenging. Sales professionals throughout the world are paying tens of millions of dollars for this advice by taking ongoing training. The bottom line is executing in the marketplace, and that would be, you guessed it - **Focus and Follow-up.**

Don't misunderstand. An effective salesperson, or sales manager, who has truly made a profession out of his or her career will invest heavily in training. They feel it complements their significant experience and the results they have achieved. But training is only the beginning.

It would be wrong to position this book as the start of turning your lawyers into salespeople. But all things are relative. By getting your lawyers proficient in the basics of sales, they will become more effective, confident and certainly a step ahead of your competition. And I think that is the sales end game in the legal world. **Be better than your competition in all areas (and this is just one more)...play to dominate, not just to win.**

Also, don't view this book as a simple training tool, one to read and then forget. It's a "quick read" to refer to often. This book should be shared with those who want to increase their sales skills and then be willing to go out and apply the basics to actual sales efforts. **Think of this book as the beginning of Just-In-Time coaching.** After a series of successful sales efforts, these basics will begin to become second nature and your team can then move on to more advanced Just-In-Time coaching techniques.

The following seven chapters clarify each step within the pursuit process. They do not have to be linear in nature. You will probably pick up bits and pieces of information on what you should include in your proposal - from the first step, Identify, and through the other steps that lead up to asking for the sale.

Even though you think you have the answers early in the sales process, please refrain from jumping to conclusions regarding the client's issues and needs. **Especially avoid the "survey of one" if possible.** The survey of one is when you talk to only one person in the target organization, and then accept their view as that of many. Accurate validation is a luxury you probably have more often than you think when you have multiple conversation points available to you. Use them or lose them.

QUESTIONS:

1. How many steps within the pursuit process do you apply today?
2. Are you still simply playing to win or to dominate?
3. When you acquire a significant new client, how long does it take to get the team together and plan for expansion?

7. Identify

A number of avenues exist to begin developing your target list. This is the beginning of the **preparation** process. Regardless of how you decide to identify your clients and targets in order to expand business, you need to take into consideration the following four areas. You will find details on how to address these areas later in this chapter:

1. Identify your most successful clients for those lawyers participating in the sales initiative. Define the criteria/ characteristics of these clients. Determine what they look like in terms of size, industry, geography, legal dept structure, and their types of needs.

2. Put together a broad list of possibilities to pursue in three areas:

   • Current clients of the sales team where opportunities may exist to expand your services

   • Cross selling opportunities

   • New-firm clients

3. Apply the criteria developed in step 1 and apply to the broad list in step 2 and prioritize your best chances of winning.

Identify

4. Define your value proposition. Determine what makes you a leading player in this space and identify your differentiators.

This activity can be as hard and time consuming as you want to make it. You can hire market experts to do it, go through a strengths/weaknesses/opportunities/threats (SWOT) analysis and apply it painstakingly to your marketplace.

Or you can follow some simple steps and then commit to continually refine your targets as experience dictates. This will give you far more room to adjust your approach, which will be critical as you move along in the sales process.

If you decide on the more simplified process, begin formulating your direction with the following steps and then continually refine your process. Ultimately, your objective is to get three manageable sets of targets in each of the following areas:

1. **Current clients of the practice group or lawyers who are participating in sales efforts where growth opportunities are evident** - The objective here is getting the quickest return on your efforts - maybe not the most dramatic or decisive, but the quickest. We will designate this activity as **service expansion**, expanding your business where you have business today.

2. **Current firm clients that are not working with the Practice Groups or group of lawyers participating in the sales effort** - The objective here is **cross selling** – to introducing new Practice Service Areas to these clients. You will not see results here as quickly as in the service

expansion effort. However, the results are generally more dramatic than service expansion and faster than new client development.

3. **New clients of your firm** - This is generally the longest sales cycle but when done correctly, gives you the most dramatic results.

We know the three areas upon which we would like to focus our efforts - **Service Expansion, Cross Selling and New Clients.** But in which of these areas should we place the most emphasis?

This decision is generally market-driven. In **slow times, Service Expansion and Cross Selling** should be the primary focus. In **prosperous times, New Client Development, along with Cross Selling,** should be emphasized. This would appear to be somewhat obvious, but in the course and heat of the battle, sometimes the obvious gets lost.

So how do we get started developing our target lists? Regardless of which of the three areas you are emphasizing, the basics are the same:

1. Have your sales team(s), identify their respective top ten best clients and top ten worst clients. List the criteria, soft and hard measures, that put them in these categories. By soft measures I mean those things that make the relationship work. Hard measures mean the demographics, such as the size of the company, the industry, location, etc. Mix and match these two lists and identify the ideal client criteria and any red flags that may identify a problem client.

Identify

Also, examine the various issues you address and services you provide, and then list them. Are there other emerging services that you should include in your client review as well?

2. Determine your value proposition. What is it that keeps your best clients coming back to you? What services do they use on a consistent basis and why do they use you?

3. Validate with clients. I don't recommend that you ask them the soft measure and value proposition questions mentioned in numbers 1 and 2 directly, but use this as part of your regular service review with your best clients, a way of gathering intelligence. *What? You don't routinely do reviews with your clients? Well, now is a good time to start.* Understanding the areas where your clients are very satisfied and recognize your value. A few of their answers may surprise you and actually get you to expand your list.

Make sure that the third area roughly matches the criteria you identified in the first two areas. If it doesn't, go back and address the differences before moving forward. It is important that you know why they do business with you. This should be clear to you, and to the client to help clarify your targets.

While talking to your clients, be sure to listen for opportunities for improvement. They will appreciate your proactive approach, and by addressing these areas, you take another step in solidifying the relationship. But a bit of caution - if they do raise areas of improvement, then you must commit to doing your best to address them. If you simply give this "lip service" and do nothing, a chance exists that you could do more harm than good in having that discussion.

4. Having had both the internal sessions and external probing conversations, you need to define, on paper, both your ideal client criteria and your value proposition. Once you have done this, apply this criterion for choosing your client targets in three areas:

    1. Ask each of your lawyers participating in this effort to apply the criteria and value proposition to their current clients. Ask that they identify seven clients where they think expansions of their business is most likely (**Service Expansion**).

    2. Ask your finance group to run the top 200 firm clients and again have your sales team apply the criteria and value proposition to this list. Identify the top seven companies where they think they can **Cross Sell,** (to firm clients with whom they are not currently doing business).

    3. The third area is pursuing new clients, **Targets**. Have your library or research group perform market analysis using the criteria you developed as filters. Then apply your value proposition to the lists and again prioritize seven companies where relationships exist.

Prioritize these companies starting with your best prospects for success. Determine where you think your value proposition will play best, and then commit to qualifying at least a third of them within the next 90 days.

QUESTIONS:

1. How well have you defined your ideal client criteria and value proposition?

2. Do you routinely prioritize your sales pursuits?

3. Does your sales strategy take into consideration the changing economic environment?

8. Qualify

This chapter continues discussing the preparation phase within the sales process, but expands the subject to include the transitional step of beginning the pursuit process. Generally, once lawyers identify targets, cross selling or service expansion opportunities, the starting point question is "what do we want to present to them?" All too often in my discussions with attorneys, their understanding of prospective clients is mostly educated guesswork. They know only bits and pieces about the company and the industry. They assume they know what the particular client is likely to need. And sometimes, they've only talked to one person, not the decision-maker, and want to use that discussion as a path to sales success.

If you had nothing else to talk to them about, this would probably be a decent approach. But you do have alternatives. Frankly, if you are familiar with this company and know that they have issues in a particular area, you would still be wrought with risk by simply doing it this way.

Think about it. You approach the client, confident that you know the issues near and dear to their heart. But any number of factors can derail your sales efforts. Unbeknownst to you, they may already have a reliable, long-term relationship with another firm in this area. Maybe they have their talented in-house lawyers handling it. Or possibly they just made a change and brought in a new law firm to handle this area. Putting your eggs, as they say, in one or even two baskets is very risky.

But what if you have a way of putting your eggs in one or two baskets that you know need filling? This chapter is about beginning to understand the baskets of opportunity that exist with your prospect before you invest the time and energy in making a sales pitch.

With a complex sale, many variables can exist. You need to be aware of them - a few of which we have already discussed. For simplicity's sake, we can narrow them down to three broad areas:

- Being company smart

- Being client smart

- Being contact smart

Let's look at all three:

COMPANY SMART

First you need to understand the basics of the company. Look at business intelligence such as their size, number of employees, their locations, corporate structure, key business units and initiatives, challenges and risks they face, and types of litigations in which they have been involved. All this information helps you better frame the company, and gives you a good overview and a feel for their operations. You can gather most of this information through basic company research from public sources.

Be careful not to over prepare in this phase. Here is a good rule of thumb regarding how much you should know about a company. Suppose this company contact asked you to give a three-minute company overview to a group of industry analysts. You wouldn't have time to go into a lot of detail, just touch upon the key facts about the company.

CLIENT SMART

As I mentioned before, you need to determine how the organization is run and how they buy legal services. No amount of public knowledge will tell you these things. Once you complete the company research, and no red flags come up, it's time to have a conversation with someone at that company. It might not be a decision-maker or key influencer, but it should be someone who knows the organization and how things work.

First you should determine whether you have any relationships within this company. If not, then the first step is to figure how to begin engaging in a relationship there. Fostering multiple relationships is the best approach. These separate and simultaneous conversations will accelerate the relationship building. A word of caution – this effort should be coordinated so there is never a perception that you're trying to make an end run around a key influencer or decision maker or your firm has a communication problem and uncoordinated.

Being client smart means finding out the inner workings of the company. Which people should you talk to and which ones should you stay away from? How should you best approach this company? How do they buy? You may run into issues and needs at this phase and you should inventory them.

Qualify

This is fine, but the main goal is to determine what it will take to move this relationship forward.

CONTACT SMART

Ask yourself how much you actually know about the decision maker and key influencers. If your contact is not the decision-maker, does the current relationship you established give you the opportunity to understand the decision-maker's and key influencer's goals? By goals, I mean both department and personal. If we know the decision maker's short-term and long-term personal goals, along with their department goals, we can figure out the best way to approach her/him, and whether we can move his or her agenda along.

When dealing with any client, preparation is key. The more you know about a contact's departmental and personal goals and issues, the more successful you will be in establishing a new relationship or expanding a current one. If you are able to successfully gather this intelligence, you have an excellent opportunity to begin moving toward an Advisory relationship.

Always be mindful that companies and industries are constantly changing. So your intelligence gathering must always be a continuous effort. Also, be alert for red flags and opportunities. As you begin to uncover facts about the client decision-maker, be sure to have your antenna up and constantly analyze whether this target will eventually become a client, and a profitable one at that.

SOME FINAL THOUGHTS

Once you have become knowledgeable regarding the company (the basics), client (how the organization operates and how they buy) and contacts (the metrics/issues/personal motivators facing the decision-maker and key influencers), you are ready to move on to the solution assessment phase.

This is how relationships are developed. Make it a point to know more than your competition in each of these areas. You will add to each of these areas as your pursuit progresses. However, early on you should have enough information to determine whether or not this client is a viable target.

Note: There is no shame in putting a pursuit on the back burner if red flags do arise. You can't go wrong by continuing to expand your circle of friends and acquaintances. You never know when something might happen with this contact/company that puts you back into the game.

QUESTIONS:

1. Do you currently address all three areas of knowledge; being company, client and contact smart?

2. Do you have a process in place to inventory knowledge gained so you don't have to constantly revisit similar discussions?

3. How often do you revisit pursuits that you have put on the back burner to ascertain if there is an event or crisis that changes circumstances (more on events and crisis later)?

9. Solution Assessment

As you begin the Solution Assessment phase, you have already done the following:

- Identified your targets

- Narrowed the targets down to a limited, manageable number to pursue

- Begun to understand how the company works

Now is the time to roll up your sleeves and go to work on the substance that you trained your entire career to do.

Part of your qualifying efforts was to identify the metrics and issues of the decision-maker and key influencers. Although you may have a good idea of their needs at this point, it would be unwise to jump right into a proposal. The first two phases, Identify and Qualify enabled you to become company, client and contact smart.

The Solution Assessment phase involves getting **issues smart, and includes five steps:**

1. Define issues

2. Define needs

Solution Assessment

3. Prioritize needs

4. Define process

5. Define success

DEFINE ISSUES

You probably uncovered a few issues as you went through the qualifying portion of your pursuit process. Now is the time to inventory this intelligence and gain as complete a picture as possible. The more issues/options you have to consider, the better decisions you will make.

However, there are times in your life when you walk into a room, restaurant, or car dealer and you immediately know that "Yes, this is it - this is what I want!" The instant "bingo" mentality works at times, but you shouldn't get carried away with the moment. Continue to filter even the most obvious opportunities, and if it looks good, then go for it and close as quickly as you can. But avoid having tunnel vision; sales pursuits are rarely as simple as they appear.

A defined, systematic approach is best for the long term. However (and this isn't just sales lore), the harder and smarter you work, the more likely a significant opportunity will come along when you least expect it. So always have your antenna up and not just listen, but try to understand.

Defining issues is about applying the information you gathered from the first two phases of the pursuit process, and then having business conversations with decision makers and key influencers to validate and refine this information. You may also uncover hidden gems in the course of the conversation.

At this point, you want to find out what's on your target's agenda. It is really as simple as that. If the person across the desk from you values your relationship, realizes you've done your homework, and feels you are a good fit, you have a good chance of getting to the meat of the conversation - their issues.

DEFINE NEEDS

Just because a client has an issue doesn't mean they have a need. Too much time is often lost chasing these issues. The client may be able to handle the particular issue in-house, or maybe they have a rock solid, ongoing relationship with another firm. Or it could be that they're just not ready to move on it.

Has this ever happened to you? While participating in an internal meeting, a company name is thrown out for discussion as having an issue in a particular area. The conversation immediately goes on for another half hour, discussing why this target should be using your firm. This exercise is often a total waste of time. Not only do you waste the half hour with two or three or more lawyers in a room but you also waste support time. The next predictable step is to have the library or marketing do research, followed by the marketing group putting together a document for the client as talking points.

At this stage, you should not be proposing and focusing in on one issue at a time with a valued contact. Instead, multiple issues in your discussions should be raised to be as efficient as possible for both you and your potential client. In an hour with a good contact, a lawyer can uncover several issues and determine where the genuine needs reside.

PRIORITIZE NEEDS

Client priorities come in three flavors:

- "Have to do"

- "Need to do"

- "Nice to do"

"Have to do's" get done. "Need to do's" get done with some pushing, both internal and external. "Nice to do's" generally never get done. If they manage to get done, they are usually under-funded, and in other words, you don't make any money.

Hopefully, you will have one or two opportunities in each area. Focus on the "have to's", then the "need to's." Only concentrate on the "nice to do's" if you need a strategic win to gain an entry into this target, and think you have no chance with the other two.

DEFINE PROCESS

This will continue to become a bigger issue as the buying of professional services become more involved with both procurement departments and General Counsel's changing metrics. Both will be pressured to act more like business people.

Validating how a company purchases services is important. I suggested that discussions in this area begin in the qualifying phase. It is important to address this, maybe not as directly as before (if you already had a good discussion), but perhaps indirectly as needed to validate.

Don't assume that what was discussed at the beginning of the pursuit process has stayed the same. Your relationship may have changed, maybe some players at the target company changed or business conditions changed. Validating the buying process at this phase is as important as validating when discussions begin. You haven't come all this way to get a surprise at the end.

DEFINE SUCCESS

An issue and need may seem perfect for you, but it's important to identify what the client is trying to accomplish and what *they* consider success. This is the last piece prior to beginning the proposal process. The client may have a totally different and conflicting idea on what the approach and outcome should be. **This is rarely a stumbling block with law firms that I have seen, but on occasion, it does pose a conflict.**

Once you determine the issue and need that you are well positioned to fill, feel the client's sense of urgency and are comfortable with the process and their idea of success, it is time to move quickly and aggressively with the proposal phase - to develop your Separation Strategy.

QUESTIONS:

1. Do your lawyers understand the difference between needs and issues?
2. Do the lawyers in your firm know how to identify needs and issues and how then to position them as opportunities?
3. Do your lawyers often get a solid understanding of the client's desired methodology prior to proposing?

10. Separation Strategy

In the first three phases of the sales process you identified your target, qualified them, and defined and prioritized the opportunities. Now is the time to follow through on a winning separation strategy.

A Separation Strategy goes beyond just trying to win. It seeks to clearly differentiate you from the competition, and not by a narrow margin. Companies that grow rapidly seek to dominate, not just win. They are truly separate and are perceived differently than their competition.

The simple and most effective approach that I have seen is to design a separation strategy that covers everyone who may have a role in the potential client's decision of which provider to engage. Those are:

- **Decision-Maker** – This person generally controls the budget. This is the value buyer.

- **Evaluation Buyer** – This individual determines if you have the credentials to successfully provide the services.

- **Contact Buyer** – This is the person you will be working closely with every day.

- **Cultural Influences** – This is the criteria that determine whether the target company and your firm are a good fit to work together.

If you can identify each of their buying criteria and then pre-sell each one (and one person may represent more than one of these buying influences) of the buyers with your points of separation, and position them as either your ally or (at the very least) a neutral party, then you win. Seldom will they all be your ally. However, if you get the decision-maker on your side and at least one other buyer, you have little chance of losing. If you have the decision-maker and at least neutralize everyone else, you win. If you don't have the decision-maker on your side, then you need at least the other three to be allies. Neutral without the decision-maker just does not get it done.

DECISION-MAKER

This person is usually the least willing to change the way things are done today. A certain comfort level exists in having a stable group of providers. Even a breakdown in client service, unless critical to the outcomes of their business, will not be a prime motivator for this person to change.

Questions about technical ability are usually handled with a call to the managing partner of the legacy provider to get the right person on the matter. The only factor to affect the relationship is if the incumbent firm is unable to help the decision-maker be successful. Does a risk exist in the current state due to changes in the client relationship or perhaps the needs and issues within the GC's organization that may drive a change? I talk about an **event or crisis** a bit later on in this chapter. This will be an indicator of whether you may have a short-term opening to gain the business.

In any pursuit, you need to understand where and how your competition fits within the decision-maker's scheme of things. How does the current provider help the decision-maker achieve his or her goals? If you are able to answer that question and then over time position yourself as the better solution than their current provider, you have a good opportunity to win the business. Often, you will find yourself replacing a secondary provider at the start, the decision maker generally is most interested in only primary providers, so understanding the current provider/prospect relationship is key. Attacking the weakest link is often the best strategy. However, realize that it is only a start. The real payoff is becoming the primary provider, the Advisory relationship. I'll explain more about that later.

EVALUATION BUYER

This person looks at two things:

- Can you get the job done?

- Are your costs in line?

Your background, experience, reputation and cost structure are all parts of the mix.

The evaluation buyer is the person of significance that you most likely meet at a conference or seminar. This person is generally second tier in influence in the General Counsel's office. Building trust quickly is very critical and can be done in a variety of ways. Your experience, mutual acquaintances, interaction in previous matters, and overall reputation within their circle of reference are all part of his or her decision criteria. It generally does not take long to get a yes or no from this person. You need to be at the right place at the right time to get your turn at the plate. Being on this person's short list, and at the top of their mind, is critical during pre-sale.

Ironically, no matter how good you are, you will never be positioned as the only game in town. This came as one of the biggest surprises to me when I began working with law firms. Many clients consider most of their legal work as commodity business. But even in non-commodity type matters, the client always feels that they have options.

CONTACT BUYER

You will work with the contact buyer day in and day out. This is the person to whom customer service is very important. She or he is one of the key people who decide whether or not you will be allowed to qualify for a long-term relationship. Obviously the first line of emphasis with this person is a successful outcome to their need. The perception of failure instantly wipes away all the client service points you score. Having success within the parameters of excellent client service keeps the contact buyer recommending you for more.

CULTURAL INFLUENCES

These are the "soft stuff" items that are inherent to the culture and values of the target company. How their people, vendors and customers are treated and the types of programs and processes they have in place support those beliefs. It is not just what they say, but what they value. That is the bottom line of what they invest in and support.

FINDING SUCCESS

I mentioned before that the proposal process means having the client determine 80 percent of your separation strategy. Here is how I have found success.

Each of the buying influencers, (Decision Maker, Evaluator, Contact and Cultural), all have their own criteria for buying. What are they looking for in a service provider? It's important to have a conversation where you discuss buying influences in the context of both relative position and objectives.

Define their key buying criteria. Getting this out of each of the buying influences is key for two reasons.

1. It gives you a sense of the contacts' priorities. You may have 10 reasons why you think they should use your services. But if you try to emphasize all 10, none may get the attention they warrant for this particular pursuit. Instead, focus on your contact's top two or three reasons to show your value and make your case.

2. It may prompt a consideration that you previously didn't have in mind.

I can't tell you how many times I have listened to a debrief conversation with a prospect following a firm loss that went something like this:

Separation Strategy

Losing Firm: *"Please help us understand why we lost the business."*

Prospect: *"Because your competitors could do XYZ."*

Losing Firm: *"Well, we can do that even better than our competition, and here's why..."*

Prospect: *"Wow. I didn't know your firm did that. But even if I knew that, I doubt it would have made a difference (this is letting you down easy – if they knew it, it would have made a difference)."*

Losing Firm: *"Well, I wish I would have known. How did our competitor know this was important to you?"*

Prospect: *"They asked."*

At this point, the conversation almost always ends.

If you can identify the key buying criteria for each influencer, then prioritize and develop a value proposition to address each of these criteria, gaining separation from your competition in key areas, you magnify your chance of success.

The key buying criteria should not be a laundry list. Instead it should be a prioritized, focused list of two or three criteria for each buying influence. If you can address each of these in a meaningful way, your chances of success are much better, especially if you have the relationship to go along with them.

How do you determine the client's top two or three buying criteria? The best way is to have a discussion with each buying influence. It is that simple. So draw it up. Name each buying influence, list their key criteria, and then fill in the best value proposition you can devise for each one, focusing on the two or three that will separate you from your competition.

NOTE: Each of these buying influences may be represented by only one or two individuals. It does not have to be four (one for each area). But be aware that your value proposition should address all four areas.

EVENT OR A CRISIS

Replacing primary providers of law services is a difficult task for law firms targeting specific companies. You have to be out there building relationships with prospects. Of course, it also helps to be at the right place at the right time.

Two things can be very helpful in increasing your odds of being at the right place at the right time - an event or crisis. Either of these can cause everything to change quickly. A change in the General Counsel is one that first comes to mind. A variety of other factors can also cause a client to consider changing providers. A major change in the company's business model, a blow-up with their current provider on a "bet the ranch" case or change in the supervising attorney can all be factors. A change in C-level management and how legal services are procured or the direction and need of different legal services can also cause significant change. Also, acquiring a substantial new entity or being acquired can cause a significant change in direction.

Be in the game with your ideal prospects and be ready to pounce when the timing and circumstances are right. Have you ever sat in a conference room and discussed a company and the whole room agreed they would never change providers? But 30 days later you find out that they did? That old saying of "they know where to find us if they need us" goes out the door. Keep your eyes and ears open for an event or crisis - your fastest track to opportunity.

One other note: You need to be at the right place at the right time but **you'll never be at the right place until you are some place.** That some place that leads to success is a matter of working smarter, and not just harder.

QUESTIONS:

1. Before proposing a major piece of business do you, as a course of the process, identify the four key buying influences?

2. Do your lawyers have an inventory of differentiators to address the different buyers, or do you make it up as you go along?

3. Do you have a means of monitoring an event or crisis with your targets, and more importantly, your clients?

11. Ask for the Sale

When asking the client for the sale, if you're not sure what the answer will be, then you really haven't done your job. Yes, we have all been surprised at times and should never take anything for granted. But at the moment of truth, you should feel very little doubt that the answer will be "yes."

Before you ask for the sale, you should have all the answers to the following checklist:

- Is this a "must-have" issue with a definitive need?

- Do you know each of the buying influences in this process?

- Do you know their business drivers, goals and objectives?

- Have you positioned your firm to help them achieve these business drivers?

- Do you know the key buying criteria for each of the influences (decision-maker, evaluator, user, cultural)?

- Have you addressed their key buying criteria and offered a solid value proposition, one that sets your firm apart from, and ahead of, your competition?

- Have you built a solid degree of trust and respect?

- Is the decision-maker an ally and everyone else either an ally or neutral?

IF YOU CAN ANSWER YES TO ALL THESE QUESTIONS THEN YOU HAVE THE SALE.

From my experience at a Big Four accounting firm, I found that these firms understood this. If a potential client, generally in an RFP situation, did not allow access to the key decision-maker and other buyers, the accounting firms looked long and hard to determine whether they should spend the time and resources to bid on the business.

You'll find that if you are not prepared prior to asking for the sale, you'll be feeling a lot of uneasiness. It starts with the uneasy feeling that maybe you missed something during the presentation. Then there's the uneasy feeling of not knowing who will actually make the buying decisions. Then you start wondering exactly who is on your side, and your firm's side, and who isn't. Then there's the uneasy feeling of the unknown relationship that may have had the inside track all along. Finally, there's the uneasy feeling of some cultural barrier that could knock you out of the game.

While you can never have 100 percent of these questions answered at the moment of truth, your win percentage will be significantly higher by simply following the basics of a separation strategy, putting some distance between you and your competition.

You have probably guessed that you should always ask for the sale. But when you get to this phase, a quality pursuit process makes asking for the order almost a non-event. The business will be awarded in the course of your pursuit process, and there will be no need to have the "big close" to get to the answer you want.

Note: If you feel you have done all the right things but you still have some questions and uncertainties, consider using a **Coach** within the organization. This person may help you get clarification on the 20 percent or so gray areas. A Coach is someone within the company with whom you trust and who understands the organization, but is not directly in the decision process. An experienced upper-middle manager is sometimes in the best position to be a Coach. They are outside the competition of the big players but high enough to understand how things work. Even if this person can't answer your question, they can usually point you in the right direction to get the answer.

QUESTIONS:

Building confidence in the sale is key.

1. For major pursuits, do you define the key buying influencers and whether they are your ally, neutral or for your competition?

2. Do you routinely identify and develop a relationship with a Coach?

3. Do you have a checklist similar to the one beginning on page 67 and a process to get to "yes" for each of the questions to help erase the uneasiness that may put you on the defensive?

12. You Won! What's Next?

Often times, lawyers will get pumped up about winning a significant piece of business but then forget that this is only one step in a continuous loop. Even though this win is important, the firm should remember to keep it in perspective with the original objective, to grow significant, recurring revenue. With so much effort spent on acquiring business, a big opportunity is wasted if you don't make the most of this sale by taking it to the next level.

Four follow-up actions should be addressed that are both critical to long-term growth and can also be handled in short order:

1. HOLD AN INTERNAL AND EXTERNAL DEBRIEF THAT IDENTIFIES WHY YOU WERE AWARDED THE BUSINESS

Often, debriefs are only held after a firm loses business. Identifying why a sale is lost is important. However, it is even more critical to understand why you were successful so you don't lose sight of what got you there in the first place. It may sound strange, but all too often something meaningful to the client is not fully recognized and appreciated by the pursuit team. Acknowledging and capturing this intelligence will enable you to use this information for a similar opportunity in the future.

Even though you won the business, you should realize that a separation strategy or its execution is rarely perfect. A successful pursuit debrief may also bring attention to areas where you can improve going forward while giving you additional insight into your competition.

2. PLAN FOR CLIENT DELIGHT

During the debrief, you should have identified the attributes of your client presentation that led to the client choosing your firm over your competition. Holding a session with your client project contacts will further emphasize how they want to be treated, as well as key satisfaction criteria for them. This intelligence should be related to your entire team even if they are not directly involved in the project.

Remember to tread lightly if you find that a decision-maker was primarily responsible for your firm getting the business. Don't get overconfident, particularly if that decision was over the objection of one or two of the other key influencers.

BE RESPECTFUL TO ALL.

As a Senior Account Manager at a marketing and sales consulting services firm, our team routinely won 80 percent of the business in our space with the area's biggest client. Our team knew the client's personnel and their customers better than many people at the company itself. To a competitor, this solid relationship was very difficult to measure and overcome.

One very frustrated competitor decided to take advantage of an event evolving in the corporate world - a centralized purchasing function that was beginning to influence the purchase of professional services. By turning their attention to this procurement department, they ended two years of frustration and eventually won a piece of business. The problem was, it was their one and only piece of significant business. They focused their entire separation strategy on getting to a key influencer in the procurement department. This person persisted and eventually got the CFO's attention, who then suggested to my contacts, (as in "I won't cut your budget") that they should award a piece of business to my competitor.

This competitor continued to focus on the purchasing department, trying to replicate the success they had the first time around. In the meantime, the evaluator and daily contacts did not like that the firm went around them to get the first piece of business. Compounding the problem, they felt the competitor did not show them the respect they warranted in the post-sales process. This relationship "faux pas" set up the competitor for failure. How they treated the evaluator and contacts assured that the new guy on the block would fail and be positioned as not being able to deliver on their promises. They became a "one hit wonder."

The sad part was that my peer at this competing firm, after three years of effort and one decent success failed to win additional business. As a result, when his management became aware of the situation, he was fired. Euphoria turned to hopelessness very quickly. The competitor paid the price of a flawed post-win strategy.

You Won! What's Next?

I mention this now because a flawed pursuit process, in spite of a short-term success, may disqualify you from future business. Make sure that all the buying influences are covered for both pre- and post-sale.

3. HOLD AN INTERNAL MEETING TO DETERMINE IF, AND WHERE, FUTURE OPPORTUNITIES MAY EXIST

I am not suggesting that right after a big win you go out and ask for more business. But now is the time to determine the kinds of future business that may be available to you. At this point, the sales process starts all over again. Here are some thought starters:

- Begin to identify where future opportunities exist and start qualifying them.

- Ask yourself what type of information can/should be gathered subtly to build your case.

- Who do you need to validate the above information?

- Think about the solution assessment - specifically the client's needs and issues, and where your firm can bring value.

- Determine a separation strategy - identify the users, decision-makers, evaluators and cultural buyers and have you positively influenced their opinion of your firm?

- Determine the appropriate time to ask for the sale. However, keep in mind, even if you are doing all this to perfection, a dissatisfied client will negate any future

business. So never lose sight of your first priority, to
satisfy the client.

4. BUILD CLIENT RELATIONSHIPS AT KEY LEVELS

Firms can often overlook that building client relationships
requires ongoing effort, tending to rely on current contacts to
help us carry the mail. Assumptions can be dangerous. Our
client contacts can provide introductions and opportunities for
new business, but you need to make the effort to touch all the
same bases that you did on the first sale.

You can't rely on the same set of circumstances to be in place
as you move from one opportunity to the next. You have to
identify key decision points for each area, and then address
each one as a stand-alone opportunity. As such, you may need
to build bridges of awareness and trust with others within an
organization and understand their unique set of buying preju-
dices and criteria.

**This has to happen before the next opportunity presents
itself.** If you only show up when opportunities become
apparent, you will be seen as a Johnny Come Lately. The new
contact may be thinking "those lawyers from that firm have
been around for two years and never spoke to me but now
that I have a piece of business for them…" - you can finish
this sentence.

You and your firm need to make the conscious decision to
take appropriate action steps to deepen the business relationships with the client. The fact that you won business should
take the client relationship to a solid Warm. The challenge is

getting to an Advisory relationship. And the only real way of doing that is to continuously build the relationship, both your breadth and depth; horizontally and vertically.

QUESTIONS:

1. Do you debrief after a key win and inventory why you won?

2. How long after a win do you begin planning for additional revenue?

3. After a win, do you focus on developing relationships with the people who supported your competitors, or do you try to avoid them?

13. You Lost the Sale. What's Next?

No one likes to lose – especially when it comes to a sales pursuit. You might want to chalk it up to bad luck or timing. But the best, most effective approach is to find out exactly what went wrong, and then avoid making those same mistakes in the future.

To do this properly, it is best to retrace your steps within the sales process. This means gathering intelligence from a number of sources. Some of the best information might come directly from the client that "got away."

Be specific to their key decision criteria and where you fell short. Any potential client not willing to give you a reasonable amount of time to debrief (after you spent a considerable amount of time preparing a proposal and all that goes with it), is probably not worth pursuing in the long run! Also, this is a clear sign that they are looking for a one-sided relationship, not a long-term, successful one.

Their honest input will be both a great help and learning experience. You can also debrief with trusted contacts and others who can provide you with different points of view. And of course, ask your team to be brutally honest with themselves. It's not an easy process, but it will pay off for future pursuits.

You Lost the Sale. What's Next?

Plus it shows this client that you really care about refining your sales process.

To recap, ask yourself the following questions:

- Did this client match our ideal client profile? Or were they a mismatch that might have doomed the firm from the beginning?

- Did you qualify them correctly? Were there red flags that were missed?

- Did you focus on the right issues and needs?

- Did you understand the key buying criteria and were you able to define a compelling value proposition?

- Did you struggle with the separation strategy? Were you uncomfortable until the end as to who provided support and who didn't?

Failure to get the business can have any number of causes. Maybe it was fees. Maybe they have an existing relationship with another firm. Maybe you did not address their key buying criteria. Most often than not, it isn't what you do, but what you **fail** to do that becomes the key component of failure. Generally, the root cause of a failed strategy is the inability to ask the right questions during the pursuit process.

Once you get a good handle on why you lost the business, consider this loss as a positive learning experience. Pointing fingers and assigning blame will only alienate your prospect and deflate your team's morale.

Once you know why you lost, the decision has to made whether you can fix the problem. **A flawed process can probably be fixed. A flawed target cannot and is best not to pursue in the future.** By gathering honest intelligence, you will be able to decide whether this client should be pursued again or simply chalked up as a learning experience.

QUESTIONS:

1. Do you routinely debrief after a loss?
2. Are you able to differentiate between a flawed pursuit and a flawed target?
3. Do you track the "whys" in pursuits you have lost and use this as a basis to apply changes in tactics throughout your firm on a proactive basis?

14. Putting Together the Program – Elements of Success

We have talked about Preparation, Pursuit and Proliferation and the individual steps within the sales process. Here are some basics that will help maintain program success over a long period of time. As you reinforce the process and begin to expand to additional areas of your firm and teams, keep in mind that any solid sales initiative consists of four elements:

1. AWARENESS

In order to initiate focus you must have clarity on what it is you want. **If people don't know what you want...should they be expected to do it?** Just going out and having some meetings will not do it. Talk about what your expectations are and what roles you would like your people to play; senior partners, junior partners, senior associates, junior associates and staff. Beyond that, what are your goals and objectives of your sales program?

2. ABILITY – TRAINING / COACHING

To avoid a lot of confusion and frustration, some form of preparation is necessary. Your lawyers are not professional salespeople, so I would avoid any type of formal sales training.

If you do, you will invest a great deal of time and effort and, most likely, two weeks after the training they will forget what they learned.

Most experienced professionals learn by being coached and then by doing. You will need some ongoing, **Just-In-Time coaching** by someone who understands your firm, sales and your client base. After a period of time, the cumulative effect of lessons learned and Just-In-Time coaching will build, enabling your team to approach sales much like they do a litigation matter. They will be able to probe, bring in subject matter experts (SMEs) to help build their case, gain an edge, execute the plan and then move on to the next opportunity.

Once you get the sales process down, it is like anything else they do. They may not remember all the nuances of each phase of the process. However, they will become familiar enough to learn to work with the process, along with what they already know and with the resources in the firm (SMEs – sales and marketing) providing assistance. When you get this combination working, a successful sales pursuit starts to come together quickly and often.

3. REWARDS / RECOGNITION

What gets rewarded gets done. This is a tough concept for law firms, as most are locked into a rather rigid compensation program. Adjusting to a different concept and reinforcing new behavior is difficult and more of an evolutionary process. If you are a firm that already rewards people for bringing in new business, your current system will complement your sales efforts well.

If your firm rewards lawyers primarily for billable hours, and not for bringing in new business or cross-selling other practice group services, then your job will be more difficult as you jump start a sales process.

Since rewards and compensation are not always the answer, perhaps recognition may be a way to supplement your efforts until your compensation plan aligns with your business acquisition strategies. Leadership's recognition of successful lawyer efforts raises the visibility of the program and builds on success and peer pressure. Various communication mediums, as well as mentions during high-level meetings, may be a means of providing this recognition. Another great approach is the consideration of sales success in a year-end ratings review.

4. MEASUREMENT AND FEEDBACK

There is that old saying that "**if you can't measure it you can't manage it.**" Communicating early and often, at least in a macro sense, and on a limited number of metrics, can build toward your ultimate goal. Not only does this help you manage the process, it serves as both a reminder and motivator for getting things done. No one likes to hear about bad results - everyone enjoys seeing good numbers. Putting the results in print will get them in front of the firm in a substantive manner. The more you show micro results that map to individual efforts, the better your measurement and feedback will supplement the process. You simply can't launch an effort and expect it to sustain itself if you never report on the results - good or bad.

In this country, we like to keep score, whether it is athletics, academia or business. No professional sports would exist without scores. No superstars could be identified without individual statistics. No honor roles would happen without grades. If nothing else, a measurement and feedback system, even if not directly tied to their compensation, appeals to the basic need to win and be recognized.

QUESTIONS:

1. Do you employ any or all of the four basic elements of success to help accelerate results?

2. Do your compensation and / or recognition systems reward for expanding business and sales?

3. Have you identified and are you measuring success?

15. There is No "I" in Team - But There is a "Me"

The concept of a team is one of the biggest issues in accelerating sales efforts in law firms. Traditionally, lawyers did not need to regularly team with multiple counterparts within their firm. But think about what RFPs are designed to do; divide and conquer. It is that old saying, "**we will either stand together or die as individuals**".

Client relationships, as with RFPs, should be looked at from a macro basis. If each client is the ward of one individual, you are at the mercy of the strength or weakness of that individual.

Client expectations constantly change and your lawyers need to address these changes as well. Approach your clients as a cohesive team, with all members equipped with a solid understanding of the nuances of the client relationship. The broader and more diverse the relationship, the more resilient your sales effort and relationship. This will help keep your firm immune to surprises.

One other note; Beware of the "me" in team. **Nothing can hurt a sales effort faster than having a "team" win but a "me" reward.**

QUESTIONS:

1. Do you typically approach significant opportunities as teams or individuals?

2. Are wins generally positioned, recognized and rewarded as a team or individual win?

3. Once you acquire a new client, is it perceived as the client of an individual or of the firm?

16. Other Items of Interest in a Sales Process

TRANSPORTABLE AND SCALABLE

As you design your sales process, take some time to ask yourself, regardless of your starting point, whether this effort will be transportable throughout your firm. Is it scalable, and able to be done on a broad basis? Think of all the effort that goes into launching a sales process. You don't want to start from scratch each time you widen the process.

You will start off with a sales initiative that is directed at a select practice group, market or even just a few prime partners. Think about the process you want them to adopt. Be sure that you can easily transport this process to other partners, practice groups or markets. Also, make sure that this process will not falter due to the size to which you plan to expand.

You don't want to find yourself starting over many times and creating confusion throughout the firm with differing processes and terminology. There's no need to work against yourself from the get-go.

"LIFE HAPPENS WHILE YOU ARE PLANNING"

This is one of my favorite quotes for all of us who plan for a living. A sales process is designed to provide focus and an efficient system for following up. However, some of your best opportunities will arise when and where you least expect it. Your lawyers need to be aware and always have their listening skills in play to take advantage of these opportunities. If we simply put on blinders, pursue our mission and lose sense of what is around us, we miss the chance for this incremental upside to our efforts. No matter how good the plan, always try to understand what the cues are for upside potential.

IT IS BETTER TO BE LUCKY THAN SMART... BUT THE HARDER/SMARTER I WORK, THE LUCKIER I GET

Any salesperson will tell you that it's better to be lucky than smart. But if you are not an active participant in the game, by working hard and smart, you will never get lucky. This kind of goes with *"Life happens while you are planning" (and doing)*. If you never get in the game, you won't have a chance of being good or lucky. These are just things in nature that seem to work well together.

IF IT IS STABLE, IT IS STALE

Don't let your program fall into a rut. Don't make changes just for the sake of change. Just as any relationship in your life needs to be energized at times, a sales effort will need to be refreshed from time to time. Not to worry though. If you commit to the sales process and give it the mind share it deserves, and you reach out to trusted firm members and advisory consultants, the ideas will naturally flow to keep the process alive and moving forward. Embrace opportunities to re-energize the process as they present themselves.

UTILIZING CONSULTANTS

There's nothing wrong with using consultants. You wouldn't expect your trusted clients to go through an acquisition without legal advice. Adding or supplementing a sales dimension at your firm is, in essence, an acquisition of a new support group. I would advise utilizing someone with the strategic background to help you design and deploy your sales initiative. They should also have the significant practical and tactical experience of having done it. This is a very rare combination, but something you need to address to accelerate acceptance of the sales function within your firm.

For strategic ability, I would look for someone who under-stands the professional services; legal, accounting or consulting industries, and who has a good sense of how a partnership / law firm works. Also, they should have the ability to talk to the big picture and then effectively work their way down.

QUESTIONS:

1. Are your sales efforts to date transportable and scalable?
2. Do you treat your sales efforts as any relationship, in need of an occasional refresh?
3. Have you used a "sales" consultant much like a client uses your law firm or are you doing it in-house?

Conclusion

Well, your introduction to **Accelerating Business Development** by incorporating **Sales** at your law firm has come to an end. Hopefully this book will instill the confidence and foundation necessary for you to go out and accelerate doing the right things regarding your sales initiative. Today, time is on your side. The thought of a successful sales process at a law firm is still a new concept. But this newness won't last forever.

IF YOU HAPPEN TO DO THE RIGHT THINGS, THEN THE RIGHT THINGS WILL HAPPEN.

Basically, the art of sales is based on doing the right activities in a focused and disciplined manner. If you ask the right questions while listening (understanding) to the responses, and offer a solid commitment to growing the client relationship, your revenue will grow.

Thank you for taking the time to read this book. For getting this far I will reward you with the answers to the questions at the end of this chapter.

Good luck and good selling.

Conclusion

QUESTIONS:

1. What are the two main concepts I should remember above all from this book? *Focus and Follow-up*

2. What is the key driver in growing my revenue? *Relationships*

3. To do things the same way, is to accept the same results, true or false? *True*

Biography

Rick Santangelo has been in sales his entire career with over twenty years in professional services sales and business development.

He spent the first seven years of his career with consumer product companies, Oscar Mayer & Co. and Texas Instruments as a District and Area Sales Manager respectively.

Since then he has held executive sales and account management positions within three professional services industries. He has worked with Maritz, Inc., consulting with Fortune 500 sales and marketing departments, Ernst & Young, a Big 4 accounting firm and Thompson Hine, an AmLaw 200 Midwest law firm.

He has been a member of LMA (Legal Marketing Association) and LSSO (Legal Sales and Service Association).

Most importantly, he has taken the past four years and applied the basics of sales success in other professional services industries and adapted it successfully to the legal industry.

www.ingramcontent.com/pod-product-compliance
Lightning Source LLC
Chambersburg PA
CBHW022102170526
45157CB00004B/1443